Contemporary

Foundations

Writing

Skill Workbook

McGraw Hill Education

Contents

MHEonline.com

Copyright © McGraw-Hill Education

Send all inquiries to:
McGraw-Hill Education
8787 Orion Place
Columbus, OH 43240

ISBN: 978-0-07-654862-0
MHID: 0-07-654862-7
Printed in the United States of America.

3 4 5 6 7 8 9 10 11 QVS 20 19 18 17 16 15 14

Descriptive Essay

Read the passage and fill in the chart.

The Peace Garden

The garden I recently visited in Florida is a peaceful place. I recommend it to anyone who needs to have a little quiet time. I would love to return there soon for another afternoon.

Before I pushed open the gate, I heard a fountain bubbling. Once inside, I could hear birds chirping at the wooden birdfeeder. Near the entrance, I saw a carved statue of an angel. I also noticed a pond where several large goldfish were swimming lazily. White and yellow lilies floated on the pond's surface. I followed a path that led beside the pond. The air was filled with the fragrance of brightly colored flowers and blooming trees. I had never smelled jasmine before, but I will never forget its sweet smell.

At the end of the path, lining the edge of the pond, were two benches. I chose to sit on the stone bench that was under a tall palm tree. No one was around. I took a deep breath and could almost taste the peace. That afternoon was the high point of my vacation.

Main Idea: overall impression	
Descriptive Details: sounds	
Descriptive Detail: sights	
Descriptive Detail: smells	
Order of details	

Descriptive Essay

Read the passage and fill in the graphic organizer.

Morning at the Farmer's Market

Walking to the Saturday morning farmer's market is my weekly treat. From a block away, I can see the blue-and-white striped tents where local farmers sell their produce and freshly baked goods. As I get closer, I can smell meat cooking at the barbeque stand. Then, I see the fruits and vegetables piled up in colorful mounds. One farmer has red, green, and yellow apples. Another has orange, green, and red peppers. Cucumbers sit beside tomatoes. There are also beets, potatoes, onions, celery, and beans.

I make my way through the stands, talking with the farmers and chatting with other customers. One man tells me he began growing heirloom tomatoes as a hobby. His tomatoes are purple, pink, yellow, orange, and green. Some are small cherry tomatoes, some fit nicely in the palm of my hand, and some weigh more than a pound.

I buy yellow tomatoes, purple eggplant, red onions, and green peppers. Tonight I will enjoy an Italian meal. It will be a colorful feast for all my senses.

Main Idea

_____

_____

Descriptive Detail

_____
_____
_____
_____
_____
_____
_____
_____

Sense: _____

Descriptive Detail

_____
_____
_____
_____
_____
_____
_____
_____

Sense: _____

Descriptive Detail

_____
_____
_____
_____
_____
_____
_____
_____

Sense: _____

Descriptive Essay

Read the passage and answer the questions.

A Strange Room

Tuesday evening was the beginning of my newest adventure. I arrived at an old brick house a few minutes before seven, parked my car, and went to the front door. I nervously rang the doorbell and then heard a cheerful voice call out, "Come in!"

I pushed open the heavy door. Then I walked into the strangest living room that I had ever seen. It had no sofa, television, or coffee table, as I would have expected. Instead, sewing machines filled the room. The machines sat on eight small tables. A padded folding chair stood behind each table. To my right, a wooden staircase led to the next floor. I could hear a radio playing in the distance. In the center of the room, under a hanging lamp, stood an ironing board ready to be used. An open cabinet stretched all along the wall to my left, under the windows. On its shelves were bolts of fabric.

A large woman wearing a flowered dress welcomed me. I could smell the coffee she was brewing in the kitchen. Her white hair was pulled back into a tight bun. Tiny half-glasses hung around her neck on a beaded chain. I was just in time for Grace's sewing class.

1. How are the details in this passage arranged?

_____

2. Which senses does this passage appeal to?

_____

3. What is missing from the living room?

_____

4. What is the most unexpected thing that the speaker sees?

_____

5. Why did the room look the way it did?

_____

Narrative Essay

Read the passage. Then answer the questions.

The Cat's Second Life

There is a reason people say that cats have nine lives. My cat, Ming, started her "second life" last week after I nearly killed her. She had gotten into some dirt and had picked up some fleas. I decided to give Ming a flea dip, though I knew that wouldn't be easy. My roommate had recently treated her dog for fleas, so I took her flea dip from the shelf and started to work.

Only after I was finished did I read the directions on the bottle. Below the directions was a warning: "Do not use on cats!" The warning was written in red letters. I panicked and called the vet. He told me to feed Ming some milk and hope she would throw up. He didn't offer me very much hope. The flea dip was deadly to cats.

Ming was angry about being wet. She shivered while I got her wrapped in a towel. I tried to get milk down her throat, but I wasn't very successful. I cried, and Ming did too. Finally, she drank a little. Then she threw up. A few hours later, my tough kitty was fine. I learned that day that I should always read the directions before beginning a project!

Part A

1. What was the narrator's problem?

   _____

2. What lesson did the narrator learn?

   _____

   _____

Part B Place the following events in correct time order. Number the first event 1, the second 2, and so on.

_____ Finally, she drank a little.

_____ I cried, and Ming did too.

_____ A few hours later, my tough kitty was fine.

_____ I decided to give Ming a flea dip.

_____ Then she threw up.

_____ I called the vet.

Narrative Essay

Read the passage and answer the questions.

Speaking Up

Kenisha had always been very shy. She never spoke up in class. Teachers quickly learned that she wouldn't answer questions, and they stopped calling on her. She did all her homework, however, and she passed all her tests.

When Kenisha began high school, she decided she had to overcome her shyness, but she wasn't sure how she could do that. Then she saw a flier announcing auditions for the school play. That was it! Maybe she could learn to speak up if she was saying words that someone else had written. At the audition, Kenisha shook with fear. Her voice could hardly be heard, and she was afraid to look up from the script. She knew she hadn't done well enough to get a part in the play.

The director was very kind. She asked Kenisha to stay after the audition. She offered Kenisha a chance to help construct the sets for the play. Kenisha surprised herself by agreeing. She had never built anything, but she started to work. Members of the stage crew had to work together, so Kenisha started talking as she worked. Before long she started talking a little in class too.

When auditions for the spring play were announced, Kenisha tried out again for a part. This time she was cast in a small role. She was on her way! She might never be a star, but she would never again be afraid to talk.

1. What is the central conflict in the passage? _____

_____

2. What kind of conflict is this? _____

3. What life lesson did Kenisha learn? _____

_____

4. Why did Kenisha think that being in a play would help her talk with others?

_____

5. How did the director help Kenisha? _____

6. How did working on sets give Kenisha more confidence? _____

_____

Narrative Essay

Read the passage and answer the questions.

Solving a Tough Problem

My supervisor, Jim, was always bumping into the women who worked at our store. His long arms brushed against us in the narrow aisles. He always said, "Oh, excuse me," but it seemed as if he was bumping into us deliberately.

I complained to the boss, but it did no good. "Jim means no harm," Mr. Browning assured me. Finally, my coworker Melinda confronted Jim one day after his hand brushed against her back. He seemed honestly puzzled by what she was saying.

From that day on, though, Jim made sure to keep his hands and arms close to his sides. He was very cold to all of us women for a long time. At least we didn't feel as if we were being harassed. We were all glad Melinda stood up for us. We all chipped in and bought her flowers.

Part A

1. The main conflict in the story is person against _____

2. What is the conflict in the story? _____

3. What action did the narrator take? _____

4. Who finally solved the difficulty? How? _____

   _____

5. What is the life lesson in this passage? _____

   _____

Part B Place the following events in time order. Number the first event 1, the second 2, and so on.

_____ The boss refuses to believe that Jim is doing anything wrong.

_____ The women buy Melinda flowers.

_____ Jim stops bumping into the women.

_____ The narrator complains to the boss.

_____ Jim brushes against Melinda.

How-To Essay

Read the passage. Then fill in the chart.

Recycling Old Furniture

Stripping and refinishing furniture is a great recycling project. By reusing a good solid piece of furniture, you will save money. You will also keep a table, a chair, or a chest from being tossed away.

The first step is to be sure you have the right supplies. You will need a drop cloth, mask, gloves, brushes, sandpaper, stripper, and varnish. Buy the supplies you don't have at the hardware store.

Before you begin your work, cover the floor with a drop cloth. Work in fresh air if possible. Cover your nose and mouth with the mask. This will protect you from breathing in harsh fumes from the stripper and varnish. Put on gloves to protect your hands.

Next, apply the stripper. This chemical helps you strip off old layers of paint and varnish. In some cases, you will need to let the stripper sit for a while. Wipe off the old paint or finish. Then wash the wood and sand it. Begin with coarse sandpaper and use a finer-grade sandpaper when you are ready to smooth the surfaces. Finally, apply a new layer of varnish. Use a sponge or brush to apply the varnish evenly.

You may want to apply a second coat of varnish after the first coat dries. When the varnish is dry, you are ready to enjoy your new old furniture!

Main Idea	
Benefits	
Time-order transition words and phrases	
Action words	

How-To Essay

Read the passage. Then answer the questions.

Don't Waste It!

Most people end up with food waste in their kitchens. Even if you use food wisely, you will have peelings, fruit cores, eggshells, and ends of vegetables. Food waste tossed in the trash goes to a landfill or dump.

Here's a better idea—composting. When plant matter breaks down, it forms compost. This soil-like material is a natural fertilizer. Even if your only plants are in small pots, you can use compost. Compost is nature's way of recycling.

Begin with a container where you can collect food scraps. The container must have a lid so the compost will not attract pests. Add banana peels, coffee grounds, and wilted lettuce. Do not add animal products such as bones or fats.

After the container is full, add the waste to the compost bin. Occasionally turning the material adds air and speeds up the composting process. If you have space, you can make your own compost pile. It must sit off the ground at a good distance away from your house. Turn the compost pile occasionally with a rake.

Finally, after the waste material has become soil, you can spread it around plants or mix it into other soil. This natural product acts as a fertilizer. Start now. Turn food waste into something you can use.

1. What are the two benefits of composting?

   _____

   _____

   _____

2. What should NOT be added to the composting material?

   _____

3. What is the advantage of adding air to the composting material?

   _____

4. List the time-order transition words and phrases used in the passage.

   _____

5. List the action words that describe the process of composting.

   _____

   _____

Essay of Example

Read the passage. Then fill in the graphic organizer.

A True Friend

Lori has been my good friend for many years. Although we now live in different states, she is ready to help me whenever I need her.

Several years ago I moved to another city. "I'll help you move," Lori said. "Do you want help packing or unpacking?" I decided to ask Lori to help me unpack. She came to town and emptied boxes, found the right places for my belongings, and moved my furniture around. Then she made me new kitchen curtains. By the time she left, the whole house felt cozy.

Another time, Lori came to visit while I was recovering from surgery. She reorganized my kitchen cabinets while I rested. One day she drove me to a special museum exhibit that I had wanted to see. I wasn't sure I would be strong enough to go the museum, but Lori made the trip as easy as possible for me. She made sure I enjoyed the exhibit but didn't get too tired out.

Recently, Lori was in town again just at the time I was trying to find a new bookcase. We looked at secondhand stores until we found the right piece. She located a mover who could deliver the bookcase that same day. Then the two of us spent the rest of the day moving books from my old bookcase to the new one.

I know that I can always count on Lori to be there when I need her. She is a true friend.

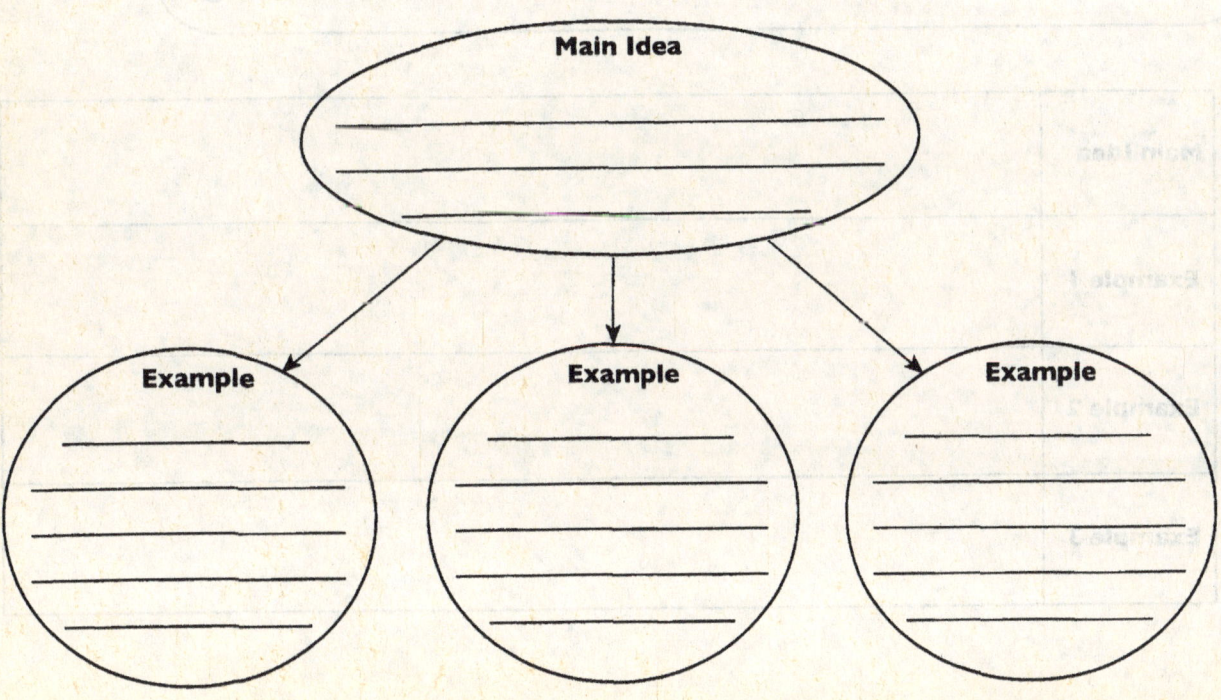

Main Idea

Example

Example

Example

Essay of Example

Read the passage and fill in the chart.

Trying to Keep Up

I am not trying to keep up with the Joneses. I'm just trying to keep up with technology. I'm finding it harder and harder to keep up-to-date, however.

First, there are the new portable media players. I was still listening to music on long-playing records when I was forced to start using cassette tapes. Then suddenly everyone was buying their music on compact discs. But now I'm behind the times again because I haven't figured out how to download music from the Internet to a portable media player.

I am also falling behind with my computer skills. Along the bottom of my computer screen are 14 icons. I know what function six of these icons will perform. I also recognize the trash-can icon. But the computer has many tools that I don't understand and have never tried using. In addition, every few days a message pops up on my computer telling me that another update is available for one software program or another. How can programs change so rapidly? Don't technology designers ever sleep?

Finally, let's talk about talking. There are cell phones, phones that take digital photos, and phones that connect to the Internet. These multitasking phones offer me too many options. I worry that I will push the wrong button and end up paying for a long-distance call!

I am not ready for this technological age. I prefer to spend my time enjoying the people I care about. I tell my friends that I'm waiting for the next version of the software. Really, though, I'm just unwilling to learn one more high-tech thing.

Main Idea	
Example 1	
Example 2	
Example 3	

Essay of Comparison and Contrast

Read the following passage and fill in the graphic organizer.

Own or Rent?

Most Americans dream of owning a home. For some people, however, renting is the wiser choice. Let's look at the facts.

If you buy a home, you gain equity as you make mortgage payments. That is, with each payment, you own a little more of the house and your lender owns a little less of it. However, if the value of your house decreases, as it did for many homeowners in 2008, you lose equity. In fact, you could end up owing your lender more than the value of the house. If you rent, you are not gaining equity. On the other hand, you will not lose equity if the house loses value.

To buy a home, you generally must make a down payment. The down payment can be several thousand dollars. Many people have not saved the large sum of money needed to make this payment. If you are renting, you may have to pay a security deposit before you can move in. This is usually equal to one or two months' rent. Sometimes this deposit is returned when you move out.

If you buy a home, you have freedoms that renters often do not have. You can paint the walls any color you want, have a pet, or plant a garden. In contrast, renters are often not allowed to do any of these things. In some cases, however, they can pay a fee in order to have a small pet.

If you live in your own home, you must be prepared to make repairs. If the hot water heater goes out, it's your responsibility. If you are renting, however, you can call the landlord, who is responsible for repairs.

All of these factors need to be considered before deciding to buy or rent your first home. Looking at each factor carefully will help you make the decision that is right for you.

Subject 1: Buying a Home		Subject 2: Renting a Home
	Basis 1: equity	
	Basis 2: money	
	Basis 3: freedoms	
	Basis 4: repairs	

Essay of Comparison and Contrast

Read the passage and then fill out the graphic organizer.

Life in the Slow Lane

At one time in my life, all I wanted to do was get where I was going—fast. I took interstate highways whenever I could. If possible, I drove about eight miles over the speed limit. Then I had to watch constantly for patrol cars so I wouldn't get a speeding ticket. Being stuck behind a semitrailer upset me. Sometimes I took risks to get around those beasts. I was also impatient when traffic slowed for long stretches of road construction. I didn't mind driving miles and miles with no signs of life. I sped along, stopping only when I needed gas or food. Usually I ate whatever food the gas station sold. At the end of a long day of frantic driving, I would arrive at a motel or a friend's house, exhausted.

Now, however, I see the benefit of taking the scenic route. I check a map for country roads that parallel the big highways. I drive the speed limit. As I enter a small town, I slow down. The slower speed gives me time to enjoy gardens and to wave at people who are out walking. I don't have diesel trucks blocking my view. The biggest vehicle I have to face is a tractor, but it is usually going only to the next farm. Road construction rarely lasts more than a short distance. I often stop at a mom-and-pop restaurant for a home-cooked meal, topped off with homemade pie. When I get to a motel or to a friend's house, I am relaxed.

Now that I have experienced both kinds of driving, I have decided that I prefer taking the more interesting route. Although I arrive a little later, time is a trade-off I am willing to make for a more pleasant day.

Basis of Comparison	Interstate Highways	Country Roads
Speed		
Big vehicles		
Road construction		
Scenery		
Food		
State of mind when arriving		

Nouns

Part A Circle the nouns in these sentences. The number at the end of each sentence tells how many nouns are in the sentence. Sometimes a noun is made up of more than one word (example: Sears Tower).

1. The Sears Tower, which rises 1,451 feet, is the tallest building in North America. (4)

2. The skyscraper is actually nine square tubes locked together so they look like one enormous building. (3)

3. Two tubes rise 49 floors, two tubes rise 65 floors, three tubes rise 90 floors, and two tubes rise 108 floors. (8)

4. Architects constructed the building in this way because of the strong winds in Chicago. (5)

5. The tower has 104 elevators and 16,100 windows. (3)

6. Six window-washing machines, which are mounted on the roof, wash the windows eight times every year. (5)

7. Water pumps are located in the basement and on the 31st, 64th, and 88th floors so water can be pumped to the top of the tower. (6)

8. The post office knows that all mail addressed to the 60606 ZIP code must be delivered to the Sears Tower. (4)

9. More than 10,000 people work in the shops, offices, and restaurants of the Sears Tower. (5)

10. About 1.5 million people visit the Skydeck on the 103rd floor each year to look out over Lake Michigan and the city of Chicago. (7)

11. Each November, more than 2,000 people climb to the top of the stairs to raise money for cancer research. (6)

12. The fastest climber went up 2,109 steps in a little more than 13 minutes. (3)

13. A Frenchman called "Spiderman" climbed the outside of the building without using any safety devices. (5)

14. The climb up the last 20 floors was difficult because fog was making the steel-and-glass walls slippery. (4)

15. Although Sears, Roebuck and Company has not owned the building for many years, it is still called the Sears Tower. (4)

Part B Capitalize all the proper nouns in these sentences.

1. The address of the tallest building in the united states is 233 south wacker drive, chicago, illinois.

2. The chief architect, bruce graham, began planning the building in 1969.

3. To build the tower, sears paid the city of chicago $2.7 million so quincy street could be closed.

4. The sears tower was opened in may 1973.

5. Today, the tallest building in the world is taipei 101 in taiwan.

Nouns: Plurals and Possessives

Part A Write the plural form of each noun.

1. potato _____
2. spy _____
3. moose _____
4. crash _____
5. author _____
6. idea _____
7. child _____
8. apple _____

9. life _____
10. deer _____
11. box _____
12. man _____
13. key _____
14. duty _____
15. loss _____
16. mouse _____

Part B Change each underlined noun to a possessive.

1. The Empire State Building is located on New York <u>City</u> Fifth Avenue.
2. From 1931 to 1972, it was the <u>world</u> tallest building.
3. The <u>building</u> height is 1,250 feet.
4. The <u>architects</u> plan for the building was completed in only two weeks.
5. The construction <u>company</u> workers included Native Americans from the Mohawk tribe.
6. The <u>Mohawks</u> reputation as ironworkers is partly due to their work on this building.
7. The <u>governor</u> grandchildren cut the ribbon to open the building, and President Hoover turned on the lights.
8. The building has been the site of many movies, and the <u>movies</u> popularity has helped make the building famous.

Extra Practice Write a short paragraph in which you use at least five of these nouns.

city   mayor's   avenues   repair   belief   feet   buses

_____

_____

_____

Pronouns

Part A Circle all the pronouns in these sentences.

1. Jackie Robinson might tell you that his first game as a Brooklyn Dodger was the most difficult baseball game he ever played.
2. At his first major league game on April 15, 1947, Dodger fans booed whenever they saw him come to bat.
3. Pitchers threw balls directly at him, and runners tried to push him out of their way.
4. Many Dodgers themselves were angry that an African American was on their team.
5. But the team manager stated, "I am the manager, and I say he plays!"
6. "You can't hate a man for his race," remarked Pee Wee Reese, the team's famous shortstop.
7. Robinson himself said, "All I ask is that you respect me as a human being."
8. In 1947, when his batting average was .342 and he had stolen 37 bases, he was named Most Valuable Player for the National League.
9. The Dodgers knew that he helped them win the World Series in 1955.
10. In 1997, the Dodgers retired uniform number 42; they said it would never be used again because it belonged to Jackie Robinson.

Part B Underline the correct pronouns in these sentences.

1. Trumpet player Louis Armstrong was famous for the way (he/him) changed the melody as (he/him) played music.
2. Armstrong liked to say, "(I/me) was born in New Orleans on the Fourth of July," but (he/him) was actually born on August 4, 1901.
3. Armstrong's mother often sent Louis and his sister to their grandmother so (her/she) could care for (they/them).
4. Louis loved the music in New Orleans restaurants where band members gave food and trumpet lessons to (he/him).
5. Mrs. Karnofsky, a Russian-born Jew, said (her/she) would loan (he/him) money so (he/him) could buy his first horn.
6. Louis and his friends earned money by singing on the streets, but what (they/them) did on the streets sometimes got (they/them) into trouble.
7. More than once Louis was sent to a home for delinquent African Americans, where the home's director said, "Louis, you can lead the band for (we/us)."
8. Later, as a young man playing trumpet on riverboats, (he/him) asked the other musicians, "Can you teach (I/me) to read music?"
9. Some people criticized (he/him) for not working harder for the Civil Rights Movement, but (he/him) supported the work of Martin Luther King Jr.
10. Although (he/him) was not well during the last few years of his life, every day Louis Armstrong said, "Let (I/me) play my trumpet."

Pronouns: Possessives

Part A Write the correct possessive pronouns on the lines. Use these pronouns.

his   her   hers   my   our   its   their

(1) Rosa Parks has been called the mother of the modern-day Civil Rights Movement because of _____ actions on an Alabama bus. (2) As a child, Parks had watched school buses take white children to _____ schools while she walked to _____. (3) In the southern United States in 1955, African Americans had to give up _____ seats on public buses if white people did not have seats. (4) The bus driver told Parks he would use _____ radio to call the police if she didn't move out of _____ seat. (5) Parks said, "I will stay in _____ seat."

* * * * * * *

(6) Thurgood Marshall is remembered for _____ success in arguing Civil Rights cases before the Supreme Court. (7) As a child, _____ father often punished him by making him read the Constitution. (8) Marshall later said, "_____ interest in law comes from that time." (9) Marshall became the first African American judge on the Supreme Court, and he helped write some of _____ most important rulings about individual rights. (10) He wanted _____ country to be a place where all people could say _____ rights were equal.

Part B Underline the correct words in these sentences.

1. (Its/It's) important that you vote if (your/you're) a U.S. citizen.
2. By voting, people are saying (their/they're) willing to work for (their/they're) country.
3. With (your/you're) vote, (your/you're) helping decide this nation's future.
4. (Its/It's) future depends on (your/you're) decision to learn about the candidates.
5. (Your/You're) vote tells candidates that (their/they're) ideas are good ones.

Extra Practice Use each of these words or phrases in a sentence.

1. my friend and I _____

2. her and him _____

3. themselves _____

4. they're_____

Verbs

Part A Circle the verbs in these sentences. The number at the end of each sentence tells how many verbs are in the sentence. Sometimes a verb is made up of more than one word (example: were racing).

1. The Iditarod Trail Sled Dog Race was started in 1973 in honor of an event that had happened in 1925 in Nome, Alaska. (2)

2. The word *Iditarod* is an Alaskan Indian word that means "distant place." (2)

3. When the town doctor saw three very sick children, the doctor realized that the children had diphtheria. (3)

4. Someone with diphtheria has a high temperature and sore throat; the illness is passed to others very easily. (2)

5. Dr. Welch told the town's mayor, "I need diphtheria serum. It will help these patients, and it will protect other people from this deadly disease." (4)

6. However, all the serum was stored 1,000 miles away in Anchorage, and it was the middle of January. (2)

7. The serum traveled 300 miles by train, and then a relay of sled-dog teams carried it to Dr. Welch. (2)

8. For six days, the sled dogs raced through a blizzard before the medicine arrived in Nome. (2)

9. Temperatures dropped below −40°, and the wind blew more than 80 miles per hour. (2)

10. The lead dog of the sled that carried the serum into Nome was Balto; today, Balto's statue stands in New York City's Central Park. (3)

Part B Underline the correct verb forms in these sentences.

1. Each March, about 65 sled-dog teams (begin/begins) the Iditarod, a 1,049-mile race over mountains, rivers, forests, and coastland.

2. Dog-sled drivers (is/are) called "mushers"; they usually (has/have) about 16 dogs pulling their sleds.

3. Each musher (carry/carries) warm clothing and an ax; the musher also (have/has) food and boots for the dogs.

4. Some mushers (run/runs) during the day, but others (do/does) their racing at night.

5. Veterinarians (check/checks) every dog so they (is/are) sure each dog (is/are) healthy enough to run for 10 to 20 days.

6. Camera crews (fly/flies) to Alaska, and they (send/sends) photos of the race all around the world.

7. When the race (begin/begins), a red lantern (is/are) hung at the finish line.

8. The last musher (take/takes) down the lantern and (blow/blows) it out; this means all the mushers (is/are) home safe.

9. Today, airplanes and snowmobiles (is/are) more common than dog sleds in Alaska.

10. The Iditarod (help/helps) Alaskans (keep/keeps) their pioneer spirit.

Verbs: Past Tense

Part A Write the past tense form of each verb.

1. climb _____
2. sing _____
3. check _____
4. eat _____
5. discover _____
6. carry _____
7. start _____
8. compare _____

9. speak _____
10. call _____
11. bury _____
12. ask _____
13. note _____
14. run _____
15. study _____
16. race _____

Part B Write the correct past tense form of the verbs in these sentences.

1. (come) Miners _____ to Alaska in the 1890s, after gold had been discovered there.

2. (begin) Soon, thousands of people _____ to arrive in Nome.

3. (bring) They _____ supplies with them on riverboats.

4. (write) Some settlers _____ letters home, encouraging friends to join them.

5. (tell) Their letters _____ of a beautiful land where the sun never sets in the summer.

6. (take) During winter, native Alaskans _____ their dogs over land and across rivers so they could buy supplies.

7. (see) The gold miners _____ that sled dogs could help them in this frozen land.

8. (go) Most of the people who _____ to Alaska did not find gold.

Extra Practice Use each of these verbs in a sentence.

1. will travel _____

2. are working _____

3. was running _____

4. will be watching _____

More About Verbs

Part A   Circle the correct verbs in these sentences.

1. The first Olympic Games (were held/had been held) 2,800 years ago in Olympia, Greece.

2. The king of one city-state (has grown/had grown) tired of all the fighting in Greece, so he (organized/has organized) a time of peace every four years.

3. Before this time of peace, the people from one city-state (have been/had been) afraid of the people from other city-states.

4. For 1,200 years, the Olympic Games (took/had taken) place in Greece every four years.

5. The modern Olympic Games (were held/have been held) since 1896.

6. More than 200 athletes from 14 countries (met/had met) in Athens, Greece, for the first modern Olympic Games.

7. Women (competed/have competed) in the games since 1900.

8. Since the first Winter Olympic Games in France in 1924, the Winter Olympics (took/have taken) place every four years.

9. In 2008, more than 10,000 athletes from 204 countries (gathered/have gathered) in Beijing, China, for 16 days of competition.

10. Swimming and gymnastics (became/have become) the most popular Olympic sports.

Part B   Write the correct verb forms on the lines.

1. (go) Native American Jim Thorpe _____ to the 1912 Olympics in Sweden.

   Thorpe _____ to practice every day for many years before he was ready for the

   Olympics. When he won gold medals for both the decathlon and the pentathlon,

   the king of Sweden said to him, "This medal _____ to the greatest athlete in

   the world."

2. (know) Before Jesse Owens went to the 1936 Olympics, he _____ that winning a

   medal would be hard work. When he arrived at the games, he _____ that Hitler,

   Germany's leader, expected white athletes to win all the medals. Today, we _____

   that Owens, an African American, won four gold medals at those Olympics.

3. (run) Because Wilma Rudolph had had polio as a little girl, she _____ for

   the first time when she was eight years old. After Rudolph _____ at the 1960

   Olympics in Rome, the newspapers reported, "She _____ like a gazelle!"

More About Verbs: Participles

Part A Underline and correct the participle error in each sentence.

1. Usain Bolt is call "Lightning" because he runs so fast.
2. At the 2008 Olympics, the record for the 100-meter race was broke by Bolt.
3. The Jamaican flag was carry around the arena by the proud runner.
4. The next day, the 200-meter race was win by Bolt.
5. In all, three gold medals were gave to Usain Bolt at the 2008 Olympics.

Part B Turn the underlined phrase into a one-word participle.

1. The gymnast <u>was injured</u> in the fall. She is an _____ gymnast.

2. The biker's tire <u>has been repaired</u>. It is a _____ tire.

3. The sailboat <u>had been damaged</u>. It was a _____ boat.

4. The swimsuit <u>was torn</u>. It is a _____ suit.

5. The swimmer's mother <u>is surprised</u>. She is a _____ mother.

Part C Circle the correct verb in each sentence.

1. Disabled athletes wanted a place where they (could competed/could compete) with the world's best disabled athletes.
2. The Olympic Committee has decided that the Paralympic Games (will take/will took) place every four years soon after the Olympic Games.
3. Paralympic athletes (may be/may been) physically or mentally handicapped.
4. They believe that they (might accomplished/might accomplish) their goals if they work hard.
5. Some disabled athletes are asking when they (can participated/can participate) in the Olympic Games.
6. One athlete with an artificial leg thinks he (would winned/would win) if he ran in the Olympics.
7. TV networks (should show/should shown) the Paralympic Games during prime time.

Extra Practice Use these words and phrases in a short paragraph in which you describe your job, your family, or your home. Be sure to use the correct verb tenses.

five years ago	last year	now	soon

_____

_____

_____

Adjectives and Adverbs

Part A Underline all the adjectives in these sentences. The number at the end of each sentence tells you how many adjectives are in the sentence.

1. The Statue of Liberty was a birthday gift from the French people to the American people in 1884. (3)
2. This well-known landmark stands in the windy harbor of New York City, more than one mile from the mainland. (4)
3. The tall lady holds a lighted torch in her right hand and a large stone tablet in her left hand. (8)
4. The 150-foot statue is copper, the torch is gold, and the base is granite. (4)
5. The Liberty Bell is older than the Statue of Liberty, and it is smaller. (2)
6. The original bell, along with many church bells, may have called the early citizens of Philadelphia to hear the first reading of the Declaration of Independence. (5)
7. The beloved bell has not rung since a large crack developed in it in 1835. (2)
8. Today, the familiar old bell stands in a beautiful new building. (4)
9. The White House is probably the most famous public building in the United States. (2)
10. Because the President's House was white, many people began calling it the "White House." (2)
11. The president and his family live in the private rooms on the second floor. (3)
12. Other rooms in this great mansion are used for official government business. (5)

Part B Circle the adverbs that describe the boldfaced words in these sentences. The questions at the end of the sentences will help you find the adverbs.

1. The most **spectacular** view in the United States may be in the Grand Canyon. (How?)
2. The Colorado River **flows** rapidly over this rocky land, and the water **has cut** deeply into the rocks. (How? How?)
3. After very **many** centuries, a canyon **was formed** there. (How many? Where?)
4. Once Native Americans **lived** there, but today no one **lives** in the main canyon. (When? Where? When?)
5. Climbing into the canyon is quite **difficult,** but people **can** easily **drive** along the rim of the canyon. (How? How?)
6. The south rim of the canyon is more frequently **visited** than the north rim. (How? When?)
7. The canyon is beautifully **colored** at sunset. (How?)
8. Tourists often **take** a dangerously **wild** ride down the river on rafts. (When? How?)
9. In winter, the winds can be bitterly **cold,** and storms **can arrive** almost instantly. (How? How? When?)
10. Park rangers **watch** protectively over the plants and animals that **live** there. (How? Where?)

Adjectives and Adverbs: Comparisons

Part A Circle the correct word or words in each sentence.

1. Washington, D.C., is a (beautiful/beautifully) city with (large/largely) monuments.
2. The Washington Monument was (careful/carefully) planned so it would be the (highest/most highly) structure in the city.
3. The Lincoln Memorial sits (peaceful/peacefully) between the Capitol and Arlington National Cemetery.
4. In 1963, Martin Luther King Jr. gave his (great/greatly) "I Have a Dream" speech at this (famous/famously) place.
5. The most (recent/recently) monument is the World War II Monument.
6. It (proud/proudly) honors the 16 million men and women who fought (courageous/courageously) from 1941 to 1945.

Part B In the blanks, write the correct form of the word in parentheses.

1. (long) When the Brooklyn Bridge was built in New York in 1883, it was the
   _____ bridge in the United States. Today, the Verrazano-Narrows Bridge in
   New York is _____ than the Brooklyn Bridge. The Golden Gate Bridge in
   San Francisco is almost as _____ as the Verrazano-Narrows Bridge.

2. (high) How _____ is Colorado's Royal Gorge Bridge? It is the _____
   bridge in the United States. It is much _____ than the Golden Gate Bridge.

3. (beautiful) Some people think the Golden Gate Bridge is the _____
   bridge in the United States. Others think the Brooklyn Bridge is _____.
   The people of Iowa think their little covered bridges are also _____.

4. (good) When early settlers wanted to build a _____ bridge, they used tree
   limbs. If they wanted to build a _____ bridge, they used lumber. When they
   used their _____ boards, they built covered bridges to protect the boards.

Extra Practice Write a short paragraph comparing two places. Include adjectives and adverbs in your descriptions. Use comparative words and phrases such as these:

        better   colder   more fun   less often

_____

_____

Sentence Structure

Part A   Add a punctuation mark to the end of each sentence.

1. Did you know that Martha Washington was never called the "First Lady"_____

2. "Lady Washington" is how she was most frequently addressed _____

3. The name "First Lady" was not used until 1849 _____

4. Dolley Madison was referred to as the "First Lady" at her funeral _____

5. What do you think the husband of a president should be called _____

Part B   Draw a slanted line between the subject and the predicate in each sentence.

1. As First Lady, Eleanor Roosevelt wrote a newspaper column six days a week.

2. She visited military bases all around the globe during World War II.

3. The young and beautiful First Lady Jacqueline Kennedy raised two small children at the White House.

4. Photos of the Kennedy family were often in magazines.

5. Hillary Rodham Clinton was the first First Lady to run for president.

Part C   Underline the coordinating conjunction (*and, but, or, nor, so*) in each sentence. Add a comma before the conjunction if the sentence is a compound sentence.

1. Martha Washington never lived in the White House but Abigail Adams did.

2. In 1814, Dolley Madison saved a famous painting of George Washington and many important papers from burning.

3. Letitia Tyler and Caroline Harrison both died while their husbands were presidents.

4. Sarah Polk worked as President Polk's secretary but earned no salary for her work.

5. The home of Mary Lincoln's grandmother was part of the Underground Railroad so enslaved people went there to hide.

6. No First Lady before Nellie Taft had either owned or driven a car.

7. Edith Wilson learned a secret military code and she translated messages for her husband during World War I.

8. Florence Harding owned a radio and flew in an airplane.

9. Bess Truman neither liked talking to reporters nor liked living in the White House.

10. Lady Bird Johnson wanted to protect the environment so she asked people to stop littering the highways.

Sentence Structure: Phrases and Clauses

Part A Correct the run-on sentences, comma splices, and sentences fragments in this paragraph.

Washington, D.C., is the capital. Of the United States. The District of Columbia is not part of any state its citizens did not have the right vote for the president until 1961. The capital city was planned by Charles L'Enfant. A French-born architect. Who had come to America to help fight in the Revolutionary War. Washington has wide avenues, they crisscross the city. Thousands of cherry trees bloom in Washington every spring thousands of tourists come to see the trees blooming. More than a half million people. That is how many people live in our nation's capital.

Part B First, underline the dependent clause in each sentence. Then add commas where they are missing.

1. The capital of the United States was New York City when George Washington was president.
2. Although the building of the White House began in 1792 it was not completed until 1800.
3. Fires that occurred in 1814 and 1929 damaged large parts of the White House.
4. President Teddy Roosevelt added tennis courts because he loved to play tennis.
5. President Franklin D. Roosevelt who had had polio built a swimming pool.
6. Roosevelt also added a movie theater that has about 40 seats.
7. When the White House was renovated in 1952 a patio was added outside the president's office.
8. A bowling alley which was built for President Harry Truman was often used by Truman's staff.
9. The president who added a jogging track was Bill Clinton.
10. The White House which is the home of the president will continue to change each time a new president is elected.

Extra Practice Write a short paragraph about a famous person or a famous place. Check carefully to be sure that all sentences are punctuated correctly.

_____

_____

_____

_____

Writing Review

Part A   Read this descriptive essay. Then identify the main idea and details.

A Perfect Evening

I recently met three old friends for dinner. The setting was lovely. Trees around the restaurant's patio had been strung with tiny white lights. As a jazz pianist played softly, we watched the sun set. Then the stars began to come out.

The food was imaginatively prepared and presented. I had a pecan-crusted pork chop. Side dishes included buttermilk-chive mashed potatoes and steamed spinach. The dessert was so huge that we split it four ways. "Chocolate Overboard"—a brownie with chocolate ice cream—was a treat!

The four of us had plenty of time to talk about our families and our work. We laughed over silly memories. It was a great evening.

Main idea: _____

Detail 1: _____

Detail 2: _____

Detail 3: _____

Part B   Read this narrative essay and answer the questions.

A Tough Battle

When my wife became pregnant, we both decided to quit smoking. We started on a Monday. I didn't realize how hard it would be for me when my coworkers took a cigarette break. However, by Wednesday I could smell their smoky clothes. I began realizing how the smell of tobacco could harm a baby's tiny lungs. On the weekend, we kept busy with projects. I cleaned out the garage, and Amy did a lot of baking. We both ate too many sweets.

Five years later, we are both smoke-free. We have two great little boys who are very healthy, and we are healthy too. We learned that love makes it easier to do the right thing.

1. What conflict does the narrator face? _____

2. Is this an internal conflict or an external conflict? _____

3. What is the climax of the story? _____

4. What lesson did the narrator and his wife learn? _____

Part C Circle the correct words in each sentence.

1. San Francisco, California, (was/has been) the site of a (terrible/terribly) disaster on April 18, 1906.

2. At 5:12 a.m., the (city/City) was awakened by a (great/greatest) earthquake.

3. One man (remember/remembers) that (he/him) was (throwed/thrown) out of bed.

4. Another man (waked/woke) up when a picture hit (he/him) on the head.

5. The earthquake (lasts/lasted) 45 (second/seconds).

6. The (violent/violently) quake (could be/could been) felt in (Oregon/Oregon,) and Nevada.

7. When the earth (shook/shook,) windows (break/broke).

8. Thousands of (chimnies/chimneys) fell (down/down,) and many people (were/had been) injured.

9. People (run/ran) into the streets so buildings would not (fall/fell) on (they/them).

10. A (child/children) called (loud/loudly), "My (sister/Sister) and (I/me) are safe."

11. In some places, the ground (cracked/has cracked) open (sudden/suddenly).

12. (Immediate/Immediately), fires (began/begun) burning throughout the (city/city,) because of (broke/broken) gas mains.

13. The (enormous/enormously) fire on Market (street/Street) was (cause/caused) by oil lamps.

14. The (fishermans'/fishermen's) boats also (catched/caught) fire.

15. The fires were (bad/worse) than the earthquake (was/had been).

16. The military (quick/quickly) started helping (people/people,) and guarding buildings.

17. No one could cook (food/food,) or use (no/any) candles.

18. Soldiers (carryed/carried) hospital patients out to the (street/Street).

19. A doctor (has written/wrote) in his diary, "A new patient was (bring/brought) to (I/me) every two minutes for two days."

20. No one wanted to waste (no/any) drops of (water/water,) because clean water was (more valuable/most valuable) than gold.

21. Although people tried (hard/hardly) to help one (another/another,) about 3,000 people (died/have died).

22. Today a scientist who (want/wants) to learn about earthquakes (may study/may studies) this 1906 quake.

Answer Key

Page 3

Main Idea: overall impression a peaceful garden

Descriptive Detail: sounds fountain bubbling, birds chirping

Descriptive Detail: sights statue, pond, goldfish, lilies, path, benches, palm tree

Descriptive Detail: smells brightly colored flowers and blooming trees, jasmine

Order of Details: outside to inside

Page 4

Main Idea: Walking to the Saturday morning farmer's market is my weekly treat.

Descriptive Detail: blue-and-white striped tents; piles of colorful fruits and vegetables

    Sense: sight

Descriptive Detail: meat cooking

    Sense: smell

Descriptive Detail: farmers and other customers talking

    Sense: sound

Page 5

1. from right to left
2. sight, sound, smell
3. sofa, television, coffee table
4. Eight sewing machines and an ironing board fill the living room.
5. It is used for a sewing class.

Page 6

Part A

1. She used a flea dip that could be deadly to her cat.
2. Always read the directions before beginning a project.

Part B

Order: 4, 3, 6, 1, 5, 2

Page 7

1. Kenisha is afraid to speak up.
2. internal conflict
3. Possible answer: Practice helps you gain skill and confidence.
4. She could speak the words others had written instead of saying her own words.
5. She asked Kenisha to join the stage crew.
6. She had to talk with others to get the job done.

Page 8

Part A

1. person
2. The women working in the store feel that Jim is harassing them.
3. She complained to the boss.
4. Melinda, one of the workers, confronted Jim.
5. Stand up for yourself.

Part B

Order: 2, 5, 4, 1, 3

Page 9

Main Idea: Stripping and refinishing furniture is a great recycling project.

Benefits: You will save money. You will also keep a table, a chair, or a chest from being tossed away.

Time-order transition words and phrases: first, before you begin, next, then, finally

Action words: buy, cover, work, put on, apply, wipe off, wash, sand, begin, use, smooth, enjoy

Page 10

1. Composting prevents waste from being added to landfills, and it provides fertilizer for plants.
2. animal products such as fats and bones
3. Air speeds up the composting process.
4. begin, after the container is full, finally
5. add, keep, make, turn, spread, mix, start

Page 11

Main Idea: Lori is a good friend.

Example: helped unpack after a move

Example: visited after surgery

Example: found and helped set up a new bookcase

Page 12

Main Idea: I cannot keep up with technology.

Example 1: music players

Example 2: computers

Example 3: phones

Page 13

Subject 1: Buying a Home		Subject 2: Renting a Home
can gain or lose equity	Basis 1: equity	never gain equity, but never lose it
possibly a large down payment	Basis 2: money	1 or 2 month's rent for a security deposit
may paint walls, own pets, plant a garden	Basis 3: freedoms	restrictions on painting, owning pets, and gardening
responsible for all repairs	Basis 4: repairs	not responsible for repairs

Page 14

Basis of Comparison	Interstate Highways	Country Roads
Speed	over the speed limit	slower
Big vehicles	semitrailers	tractors
Road construction	long stretches	short distances
Scenery	none	small towns
Food	fast-food restaurants at gas stations	mom-and-pop restaurants
State of mind when arriving	exhausted	relaxed

Page 15

Part A

1. Sears Tower, feet, building, North America
2. skyscraper, tubes, building
3. tubes, floors, tubes, floors, tubes, floors, tubes, floors
4. Architects, building, way, winds, Chicago
5. tower, elevators, windows
6. machines, roof, windows, times, year
7. pumps, basement, floors, water, top, tower
8. post office, mail, ZIP code, Sears Tower
9. people, shops, offices, restaurants, Sears Tower
10. people, Skydeck, floor, year, Lake Michigan, city, Chicago
11. November, people, top, stairs, money, research
12. climber, steps, minutes
13. Frenchman, "Spiderman," outside, building, devices
14. climb, floors, fog, walls
15. Sears, Roebuck and Company; building; years; Sears Tower

Part B

1. United States; South Wacker Drive; Chicago, Illinois
2. Bruce Graham
3. Sears; Chicago; Quincy Street
4. Sears Tower; May
5. Taipei; Taiwan

Page 16

Part A

1. potatoes
2. spies
3. moose
4. crashes
5. authors
6. ideas
7. children
8. apples
9. lives
10. deer
11. boxes
12. men
13. keys
14. duties
15. losses
16. mice

Part B

1. City's
2. world's
3. building's
4. architects'
5. company's
6. Mohawks'
7. governor's
8. movies'

Page 17

Part A

1. you, his, he
2. his, they, him
3. him, him, their
4. themselves, their
5. I, I, he
6. You, his
7. himself, I, you, me
8. his, he, he
9. he, them
10. they, it, it

Part B

1. he, he
2. I, he
3. she, them
4. him
5. she, him, he
6. they, them
7. us
8. he, me
9. him, he
10. he, me

Page 18

Part A

1. her
2. their, hers
3. their
4. his, her
5. my
6. his
7. his
8. My
9. its or our
10. our or his, their

Part B

1. It's, you're
2. they're, their
3. your, you're
4. Its, your
5. Your, their

Page 19

Part A
1. was started, had happened
2. is, means
3. saw, realized, had
4. has, is passed
5. told, need, will help, will protect
6. was stored, was
7. traveled, carried
8. raced, arrived
9. dropped, blew
10. carried, was, stands

Part B
1. begin
2. are, have
3. carries, has
4. run, do
5. check, are, is
6. fly, send
7. begins, is
8. takes, blows, are
9. are
10. helps, keep

Page 20

Part A
1. climbed
2. sang
3. checked
4. ate
5. discovered
6. carried
7. started
8. compared
9. spoke
10. called
11. buried
12. asked
13. noted
14. ran
15. studied
16. raced

Part B
1. came
2. began
3. brought
4. wrote
5. told
6. took
7. saw
8. went

Page 21

Part A
1. were held
2. had grown, organized
3. had been
4. took
5. have been held
6. met
7. have competed
8. have taken
9. gathered
10. have become

Part B
1. went, had gone, goes
2. had known, knew, know
3. ran, had run, runs

Page 22

Part A
1. called
2. broken
3. carried
4. won
5. given

Part B
1. injured
2. repaired
3. damaged
4. torn
5. surprised

Part C
1. could compete
2. will take
3. may be
4. might accomplish
5. can participate
6. would win
7. should show

Page 23

Part A
1. birthday, French, American
2. This, well-known, windy, one
3. tall, lighted, her, right, large, stone, her, left
4. 150-foot, copper, gold, granite
5. older, smaller
6. original, many, church, early, first
7. beloved, large
8. familiar, old, beautiful, new
9. famous, public
10. white, many
11. his, private, second
12. Other, this, great, official, government

Part B
1. most
2. rapidly, deeply
3. very, there
4. Once, there, today
5. quite, easily
6. more, frequently
7. beautifully
8. often, dangerously
9. bitterly, almost, instantly
10. protectively, there

Page 24

Part A
1. beautiful, large
2. carefully, highest
3. peacefully
4. great, famous
5. recent
6. proudly, courageously

Part B
1. longest; longer; long
2. high; highest; higher
3. most beautiful; more beautiful; beautiful
4. good; better; best

Page 25

Part A

1. ? 2. . 3. . 4. . 5. ?

Part B

1. Roosevelt/wrote
2. She/visited
3. Kennedy/raised
4. family/were
5. Clinton/was

Part C

1. , but
2. and
3. and
4. but
5. , so
6. or
7. , and
8. and
9. nor
10. , so

Page 26

Part A

Answers may vary.

Washington, D.C., is the capital of the United States. The District of Columbia is not part of any state. Its citizens did not have the right vote for the president until 1961. The capital city was planned by Charles L'Enfant, a French-born architect. L'Enfant had come to America to help fight in the Revolutionary War. Washington has wide avenues that crisscross the city. Thousands of cherry trees bloom in Washington every spring, and thousands of tourists come to see the trees blooming. More than a half million people live in our nation's capital.

Part B

1. when George Washington was president
2. Although the building of the White House began in 1792,
3. that occurred in 1814 and 1929
4. because he loved to play tennis
5. , who had had polio,
6. that has about 40 seats
7. When the White House was renovated in 1952,
8. , which was built for President Harry Truman,
9. who added a jogging track
10. , which is the home of the president,

Pages 27–28, Writing Review

Part A

Main Idea: Dinner with friends was memorable.

Detail 1: The setting was lovely.

Detail 2: The food was delicious.

Detail 3: The conversation was pleasant.

Part B

1. How can I quit smoking?
2. Internal—a person struggling to break a habit
3. He smells smoke on coworkers' clothes and realizes this smell will harm the baby's lungs.
4. Love makes it easier to do the right thing.

Part C

1. was — terrible
2. city — great
3. remembers — he — thrown
4. woke — him
5. lasted — seconds
6. violent — could be — Oregon
7. shook, — broke
8. chimneys — down, — were
9. ran — fall — them
10. child — loudly — sister — I
11. cracked — suddenly
12. Immediately — began — city — broken
13. enormous — Street — caused
14. fishermen's — caught
15. worse — had been
16. quickly — people
17. food — any
18. carried — street
19. wrote — brought — me
20. any — water — more valuable
21. hard — another, — died
22. wants — may study